BEFORE THE CODE

*A Primer on MoatWorks,
An AI Operating System That May
Matter More Than We Think*

BY JOHN MICHAEL KOSTAK

Pump Fake Press—Morgantown, WV

Paperback ISBN: 979-8-234-03134-1

Title: *Before the Code: A Primer on MoatWorks, An AI Operating System That May Matter More Than We Think*

Author: John Michael Kostak

Editor: Craig Irons, Irons Strategic Content, LLC

Front Cover and 7i's Marketing Mix System Art: Victoria Marinyuk

Book Design: Suzanne Reynolds

Paperback | 2026

Disclaimer: This publication contains opinions, ideas, experiences, and conceptual exercises intended for educational and informational purposes only. The reader assumes full responsibility for the use of this information. The author and publisher disclaim any liability for outcomes resulting from its application.

Dedication

For Darlene, who keeps me grounded; for our growing family; and for Luna, who has patiently walked beside me through years of long walkiwoos and longer thoughts.

7i's MARKETING SYSTEM

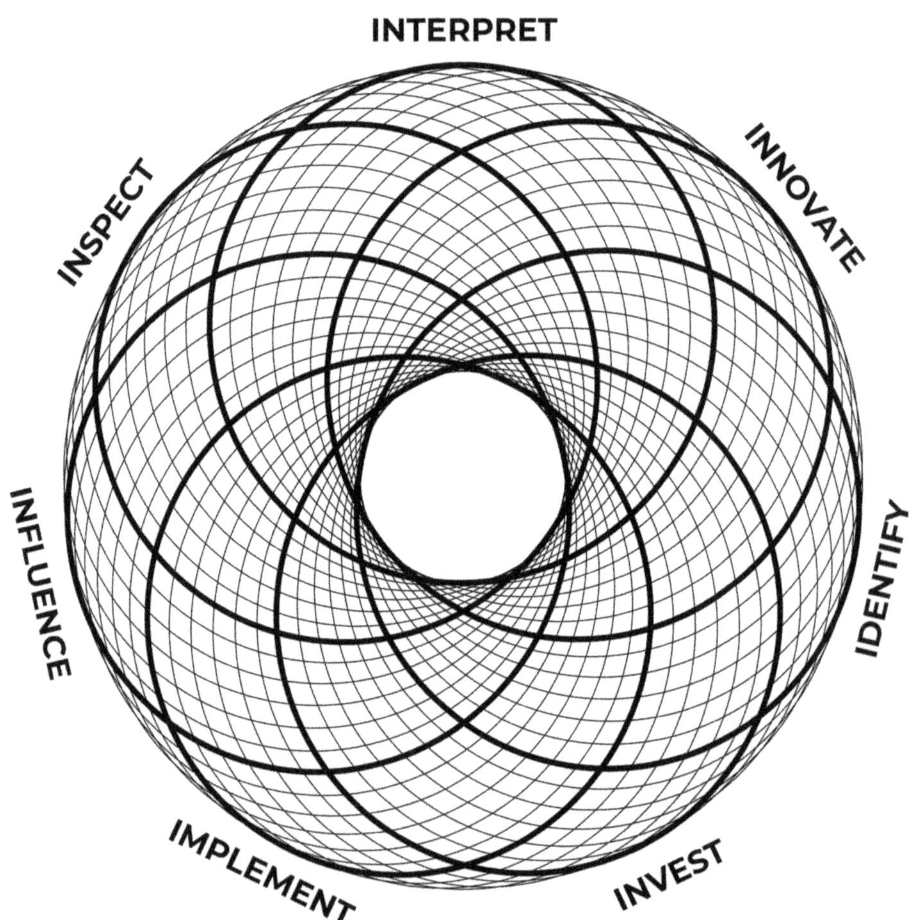

A MODERN, INTUITIVE GROWTH STRATEGY TOOL FOR BUSINESSES OF ANY SIZE

The Genesis

This work originates from the **7i's Marketing Mix System** (pronounced "Seven Eyes"), an innovative and proven strategic methodology developed to drive modernization and digital transformation. The 7i's system is an agile, iterative framework that integrates strategy, innovation, and brand management into a disciplined workflow designed to create durable competitive advantage.

This guidebook serves as a primer to the 7i's system's evolution into MoatWorks, an **AI-enabled operating system.**

Table of Contents

Foreword by Dr. Mikah Sellers

Workforce Futurist
Founder, Empathos Consulting
Author of Forging Emotionally Intelligent Leaders in the Age of AI
Co-Host, Forces of Change Podcast

When I teach leadership in the age of AI, I always ask the same question: What problem are you trying to solve? Most leaders can answer it. Far fewer can explain the system they're building to solve it consistently, over time, and at scale. That gap is the crisis hiding inside the AI boom.

Execution has become cheap. Thinking has become scarce. The tools arrived before the frameworks to govern them, and the result is a generation of leaders deploying AI without a system to compound it.

I have spent the better part of a decade studying this problem. In my book, *Forging Emotionally Intelligent Leaders in the Age of AI*, I argued that the defining leadership challenge of our era isn't technological. It's human. Emotional intelligence isn't a soft counterweight to artificial intelligence. It's the load-bearing foundation beneath it.

My *Web of Minds*, blog series, then traced that argument into the architecture of AI itself, and the pattern was consistent: the organizations most at risk are not those with too little AI. It's those deploying it without a governing system. Intelligence without architecture isn't an asset. It's liability at scale.

Before the Code is the governing system most leaders are missing. John Kostak has done something most AI practitioners resist: he slowed down long enough to think before building. The 7i's framework and its evolution into MoatWorks isn't a product pitch dressed as methodology. It's a serious attempt to answer the hardest question in enterprise AI: What is the system that surrounds the intelligence? What are the interpretive loops, the investment logic, and the implementation discipline that make AI compound rather than decay?

The central insight here is one I have seen validated across every successful transformation I have studied or led. The leaders who got it right did not start with the tool. They started with clarity about what they were trying to protect, build, and sustain. Moats are not discovered after the fact. They're designed on purpose.

Read this primer as it was intended: not as a preview of software, but as a discipline for thinking. The code will come. What matters now is whether your strategy is ready to govern it.

Eyes forward. Into the arena.

Foreword by Dr. Pablo Molina

Higher Education Technology & AI Governance Leader
Interim CIO, AVP & CISO, Drexel University
Adjunct Professor, Georgetown University
Board Member, Center for AI and Digital Policy

Foreword, forewarned, forearmed

In *Before the Code*, John Kostak enthusiastically unveils an original model to create organizational value. His 7i's Marketing Mix System crystallizes a deep understanding of digital transformation and marketing with sharp critical thinking. His proposal is strategic, systemic, integrated, pervasive, persistent, and cumulative. It aims to provide a sustainable competitive advantage when the information technology pieces — artificial intelligence tools and services, are look-alike tools.

More crudely, years ago I crafted the 6Ps approach to succeed in digital transformation: plans, people, products, policies, and processes. Wait. I am missing one: Pablo, hire Pablo or another principal to lead digital transformation. Models like John Kostak's, others', and mine help us make sense of complex environments, manage organizations, and influence human behavior.

I believe in principles. I believe in principles to guide human behavior, to support our morality. I believe in principle-centered leadership. I believe in principle-based technology adoption, (e.g., privacy by design or information security by design). In 2018, many of us in industry, civil society, and academia wrote and signed the Universal Guidelines for AI, therefore inspiring many other declarations, from the Vatican's to the Organisation for Economic Co-operation and

Development's, from Meta's to Google's.

Information technology governance in general, and AI governance in particular, tries to maximize value from implementing technologies while curtailing the abuses. John Kostak's primer is an ingenious blueprint to do so. Governance isn't an obstacle to implementation, but what reduces the risk of implementations running amok. Without information technology governance, organizational improvements, economic efficiencies, and moral integrity are elusive.

The author is clear: this primer is meant for Fortune 2000 organizations. However, could some of these ideas not be applied to other complex organizations, like colleges and universities, non-profits, or government agencies? A combination of creativity and laziness makes me think so. As you read these pages, reflect on where else and how the author's proposal could create organizational value. Challenge some of his ideas with counterexamples and validate others with your experience. Original ideas demand active reading. Engage intellectually with this material. I did.

Warning: No artificial intelligence entity was harmed or abused in the writing of these words.

Acknowledgments

I'm grateful to Dr. Leo Manhanga, Lloyd Charlier, and Craig Irons for their thoughtful contributions to this work. Each, in a different way, helped sharpen the thinking behind these pages—through insight, perspective, challenge, and encouragement. I deeply appreciate their generosity in helping strengthen the ideas that shaped this primer.

To the teachers and mentors who shaped my thinking— Mark Amtower, Mrs. Balgavy, Mr. Snellings, Gwen Costello, Charlie Harding, Mrs. Inman, Mr. Cox, Mr. Steiner; Professors Robert Pecore, Pradeep Rau, Pablo Molina, Mikah Sellers, and Per Lindgren; and Tom Gebler, Mitsuji Hashimoto, Stephane Johnson, Pat Conlon, and Dr. Georgio Coraluppi—my deep thanks. Each of you, in different ways, helped sharpen my judgment, expand my perspective, and influence the ideas behind this work.

1 | Primer:

Why This Publication Exists

This isn't a traditional business guidebook. It's not a methodology manual, a marketing playbook, or a catalog of tactics. It's a **primer**—written deliberately *before* the release of a software platform—to explain the logic, intent, and operating structure behind an AI operating system now being built: **MoatWorks,** by The Moat Factory.

In this era when AI models are rapidly becoming interchangeable, durable advantage no longer comes from the model alone. It comes from the *system* that surrounds it: how intelligence is gathered, how decisions are sequenced, how learning compounds, and how deeply those capabilities embed into real workflows.

MoatWorks is being built to enable these critical necessities. This guidebook explains the system's reasoning and establishes the core model *before* it's implemented in software.

What matters here is sequence. In most organizations, software arrives before shared understanding does. Teams adopt tools, launch pilots, and move quickly toward implementation, but the governing logic behind those decisions often remains fragmented or implied. The result is motion without a durable frame of reference. Initiatives may look intelligent in isolation while still weakening coherence at the system level.

This primer is written to reverse that sequence. It's meant to make the logic visible before the machinery makes it operational. It gives the reader a way to understand what is being built, what assumptions sit underneath it, and what kind of strategic discipline is required if AI is going to strengthen advantage rather than dilute it. In that sense, this guidebook is less about software announcement than strategic direction.

This distinction matters because the problem being addressed here isn't a lack of tools. It's a lack of structure around how intelligence should be interpreted, governed, connected, and turned into value that builds over time. Before a system like MoatWorks can be trusted, its worldview has to be understood. This publication exists to provide that foundation.

The Stack: Methodology, Suite, and Operating System

To be clear, we're distinguishing three layers.

1. The 7i's Methodology

A strategic operating model consisting of seven core areas governing how organizations interpret reality, design advantage, and compound learning over time.

2. The Moat Suite

Seven AI-enabled domain capabilities aligned to the 7i's methodology. Each domain produces specific decision artifacts and supports structured workflows.

3. MoatWorks

The integrated AI operating system that coordinates the Moat Suite, manages decision flows across domains, enforces governance, and embeds learning loops throughout the enterprise.

The methodology defines the logic. The suite puts the domains into practice. The operating system coordinates and governs the whole.

When considered together, these three layers explain why this publication has to begin where it does. Readers don't need a feature tour yet. They need a conceptual map. Without that map, the methodology can sound abstract, the suite can sound modular, and the operating system can sound ambitious. With it, the relationship becomes clear: a governing logic, a set of applied domain capabilities, and an integrated system designed to make those capabilities durable, inspectable, and compounding over time.

This publication explains the logic before it's encoded in software.

From Methods to Moats

For decades, growth and marketing disciplines have often been taught as linear process steps to follow, complete, and revisit (usually only when something breaks). That framing worked when markets moved slowly and execution costs were high.

It fails in an AI-saturated world.

Today, execution is cheap in a way it's never been before. Content, analysis, recommendations, and plans can be generated almost instantly. What remains scarce isn't activity, but coherent, secure direction — and the ability to compound learning over time rather than reset it with each new initiative, tool, or team. Strategic data findings and the subsequent actions to be taken will shift away from *methods* to *moats*.

That phrase deserves to be read carefully. A method tells an organization what to do. A moat changes what becomes possible to sustain. Methods can improve performance, but they're often portable. They can be copied, adapted, and deployed by others with enough speed and competence. A moat is different. It's not merely a better playbook. It's a system condition in which learning, execution, governance, and operational context begin to reinforce one another in ways that are increasingly difficult to reproduce from the outside.

This is why the shift matters so much in an AI-driven environment. When content, analysis, and even strategic recommendations can be generated instantly, the value of isolated outputs falls quickly. What holds value longer is the structure that determines how those outputs are interpreted, where they're installed, how they're governed, and whether they improve through use. In other words, advantage moves away from the visible artifact and toward the invisible system that produces, disciplines, and compounds it.

MoatWorks is designed as an operating system that unifies intelligence, data, AI, and execution into a closed-loop environment that improves continuously, embeds deeply, and becomes increasingly difficult to replace.

What We Mean by an AI Moat

At its core, an **AI moat** is what makes a system difficult to copy or replace, even by competitors with capital, talent, or access to similar models. In a world where AI technology itself is increasingly commoditized, advantage no longer comes from the model alone, but from the system that surrounds it.

Within MoatWorks, an AI moat is created when intelligence is embedded into real operations, continuously improves through use, and becomes progressively more valuable the longer it's in place.

This definition is intentionally practical. It does not treat the moat as an abstract strategic label or a branding flourish. It treats it as an operational outcome. If intelligence remains detached from real workflows, it may impress, but it doesn't defend. If it can't improve through repeated use, it may assist, but it doesn't compound. If it doesn't become more deeply woven into decision-making, accountability, and institutional memory over time, it may accelerate activity without increasing resilience—or adding real value.

An AI moat, then, isn't created at the moment of deployment. It's created through repeated use under real conditions. It's strengthened when better decisions create better data, better data improves the system, and the improved system becomes more embedded in how the organization functions. That's the compounding logic MoatWorks is meant to industrialize.

The worth of that definition becomes clearer when viewed in operational terms. If an AI moat is real, it should not appear only as a strategic claim. It should show up in the conditions the system creates inside the organization: how it learns, how it embeds, how it earns trust, and how it turns repeated use into compounding advantage. The capabilities detailed below describe those conditions in practical form.

MoatWorks Builds Advantage by Enabling Organizations To:

- **Improve continuously through proprietary feedback**
  Learning loops are captured from real decisions, outcomes, and usage — not just abstract training data — allowing the system to get smarter in ways competitors can't easily replicate.

- **Perform better in real operational context**
  Intelligence is shaped by how work gets done, not how it's imagined in theory. This produces insights and recommendations that are context-aware, practical, and trusted by operators.

- **Raise switching costs through workflow and system embedment**
  The system becomes part of how decisions are made, processes are executed, and results are measured. Replacing it would require unwinding not just software and infrastructure, but habits, workflows, and institutional knowledge.

- **Institutionalize trust, reliability, and governance**
  Decisions are explainable, auditable, and consistent. Trust compounds over time as the system proves reliable, aligned with intent, and accountable for outcomes.

- **Accumulate value at the system level, not the task level**
  Each interaction with the AI system contributes to a growing body of structured intelligence. Value compounds across domains, decisions, and cycles, rather than resetting with each new initiative or tool.

MoatWorks is purpose-built to industrialize these conditions.

Taken together, these conditions describe a system that does more than automate work. They describe a system that remembers, disciplines, and strengthens the organization as it operates. That distinction is critical. Many AI deployments can create speed. Far fewer create continuity. Fewer still create institutional learning that survives personnel changes, shifting priorities, and successive waves of tooling.

That's where a real moat begins to emerge. Not in novelty. Not in isolated efficiency. But in the steady conversion of decisions, workflows, and outcomes into structured intelligence that the organization can keep using, governing, and improving over time.

What MoatWorks Produces in Practice

Concepts alone don't create advantage. Systems do.

And systems become credible only when their logic shows up in repeatable outputs that guide action over time.

Each domain within the MoatWorks operating system produces concrete artifacts that guide decisions and preserve institutional learning.

These outputs matter because strategy only becomes

durable when it can be made visible, revisited, and improved without starting over. In most organizations, key judgments live inside presentations, meetings, and individual memory. They may influence action for a time, but they rarely persist in a form the system can learn from.

MoatWorks is designed to change that by turning strategic reasoning into structured artifacts that can be referenced across domains, tested against outcomes, and carried forward as organizational know-how. The artifacts organizations can access include:

A Strategic Point of View

A continuously updated statement of the organization's understanding of market reality, constraints, and strategic priorities.

An Option Portfolio

A structured set of viable strategic options defined by intent, capabilities required, validation criteria, and downside exposure.

An Identity and Policy Model

A clearly defined representation of the organization's positioning, value architecture, and enforceable operating constraints.

An Investment Allocation Record

Documented resource commitments, pricing structures, capital allocation decisions, and the reasoning behind them.

A Workflow Embedment Map

A system-level view of how strategy is installed into operational workflows, systems, and incentives.

A Benefit Realization Report

Measured financial and operational outcomes compared to original intent.

A Governance Audit Log

A persistent record of strategic decisions, automated actions, and system adjustments.

These artifacts transform strategy from episodic planning into a continuous operating system.

That shift is more important than it may first appear. Many strategic environments are rich in conversation but poor in continuity. Decisions are made, priorities are declared, and plans are launched, yet the logic behind them is often lost as teams change, conditions shift, or new initiatives take over. By contrast, a system that preserves strategic artifacts creates continuity of judgment. It gives the organization a way to remember not only what it decided, but why, under what assumptions, and with what results.

In that sense, these outputs are not administrative byproducts. They're the operating memory of the moat. They allow strategy to accumulate rather than evaporate, and they make inspection, adaptation, and reinvestment possible without having to reconstruct the past each time the environment changes.

A Simple Operating Snapshot

The easiest way to understand MoatWorks isn't as a diagram, but as a live operating sequence. Its value is most visible when conditions change unexpectedly, and the organization must respond without losing coherence. In those moments, the system isn't inventing strategy from scratch. It's absorbing new reality, converting that reality into disciplined choices, and pushing those choices back into the enterprise in a form that can be acted on, measured, and improved.

Imagine a sudden market shift that sharply reduces demand in a key customer segment. For many organizations, that kind of disruption triggers confusion, fragmented response, and a scramble to reconstruct context. In MoatWorks, the system isn't reacting from scratch. In the background, MoatSuite's seven AI domains have already been ingesting signals from the enterprise's AI "feeders," running domain-level analysis in real time, and continuously updating the broader Moat operating system. As a result, the organization can respond from an informed position rather than from shock.

What follows isn't a chain of isolated tool outputs. It's a coordinated response loop. Each domain performs a distinct role, but each is also dependent on the quality of what came before it and responsible for improving what comes after it. That's what makes the system cumulative rather than reactive.

INTERPRET AI Domain

Updates the Strategic Point of View using new performance data, external signals, and internal constraints.

INNOVATE AI Domain

Generates a portfolio of viable response options, each with defined upside, downside, and validation criteria.

IDENTIFY AI Domain

Clarifies the strategic position, core message, and market meaning so the business knows what it's claiming and why it matters.

INVEST AI Domain

Engineers pricing, economic design, and value creation paths that go beyond ROI and TCO to redefine customer jobs to be done, limit competition, and extend enterprise advantage.

IMPLEMENT AI Domain

Installs the strategy into operational workflows, systems, and incentives.

INFLUENCE AI Domain

Aligns messaging, activation channels, and customer engagement around the new direction.

INSPECT AI Domain

Measures results, detects early drift, and feeds updated outcomes back into the other domains.

The loop doesn't reset. Context persists and learning compounds.

That final point is the heart of the system. In most organizations, disruption forces a partial reset. Teams reinterpret conditions, reframe priorities, and rebuild context under pressure, often with incomplete memory of what was tried before and why. MoatWorks is designed to reduce that loss. By preserving reasoning, artifacts, decisions, and measured outcomes across cycles, it allows adaptation to become cumulative rather than episodic.

This is also why the operating snapshot matters in a primer like this one. It shows that the value of the system isn't confined to analysis or recommendation alone. Its value lies in continuity: the ability to move from signal to decision to implementation to inspection without losing organizational know-how along the way.

What This Publication Is and Is Not

This publication **is**:

- A conceptual foundation for an AI operating system (MoatWorks)
- A declaration of how durable advantage is engineered in an AI-native world
- A framing document for leaders, builders, and investors evaluating what comes next

This publication **is not**:

- A consulting methodology
- A substitute for judgment
- A promise that AI alone creates defensibility

The system described here assumes the opposite: That AI is only as powerful as the strategic structure that governs it.

Why a Primer, not a Manual

Software makes systems visible. Guidebooks make them intelligible.

MoatWorks intends to eventually operationalize the ideas introduced here—connecting data, workflows, and learning loops across an organization. By design, this guidebook, as a primer, stops short of getting into deep descriptions of these ideas or providing guidance or specifics for using the Moat-Works AI operating system.

Instead, the role of this publication is to set the stage and align expectations to ensure that when the software arrives, it feels inevitable rather than surprising.

That's the purpose of a primer.

2 | Introduction:

Designing Advantage Before the Code

Most organizations today experience strategy as reaction. While they may set expectations and direction at the outset, these best-laid plans get trampled by the demands of disruption. Platforms change. Competitive pressure shifts. Teams adapt quickly, but rarely coherently.

The result is motion without accumulation.

AI accelerates this problem as much as it promises to solve it. Without a governing system, intelligence becomes fragmented, insights are forgotten, and each new initiative begins as if the last one never happened.

The decision facing most companies is no longer whether to use AI, but **how to design systems where AI compounds advantage rather than amplifying noise.** And when an organization and its brands represent millions — or billions — of dollars in IP, valuation, and equity, stewardship demands more: the decision must also include **how to protect the system itself, and the AI embedded within it.**

This is the point at which the conversation has to mature. For years, digital transformation was often framed as one or more questions of adoption: Which platforms to buy? Which processes to automate? Which capabilities to modernize?

AI changes that framing. It forces a deeper question beneath adoption itself: What's the governing logic that determines how intelligence is used? How is it constrained? And how is its value is preserved rather than leaked into the market?

Without that thinking, speed can create risk. With it, intelligence has a chance to become a mounting asset rather than a threat.

The Real Problem and the Real Opportunity

This work sits at the highest intersection of modern marketing, enterprise strategy, and applied artificial intelligence, where marketing becomes a system of intelligence, technology becomes a governor of growth, and AI becomes an operating layer rather than a collection of tools.

For more than 75 years, organizations learned, often painfully, that growth without discipline destroys value. From Deming and Juran's quality revolutions, to Kotler's formalization of marketing, to lean, continuous improvement, and brand stewardship, one principle endured: **advantage must be designed as a system**.

As enterprise technology matured, consulting and integration firms helped organizations scale through CRM, ERP, marketing operations, analytics, and middleware. Efficiency improved. Automation expanded. But innovation slowly gave way to optimization. Best practices became safe practices. Differentiation eroded.

That erosion did not happen because organizations stopped trying. It happened because the systems they adopted were primarily designed to scale known functions, not to continuously re-interpret advantage under changing conditions. Over time, execution became more disciplined, but strategic imagination became narrower. Organizations got better at running the machine they had, even as the market increasingly demanded the ability to rethink the machine itself.

The **7i's methodology** emerged as a pragmatic response to this erosion: an agile, iterative, 360-degree growth system designed not merely to optimize activity, but to help organizations modernize, innovate inexpensively, and evolve under restrictions.

That was when time was still on their side. **AI has now removed that luxury.**

AI doesn't merely accelerate execution—it collapses reaction time. The risks that once unfolded over years now compound in quarters or weeks. Strategic drift becomes immediate exposure. Poor decisions are no longer isolated; they're amplified, learned, replicated, and scaled.

AI isn't dangerous. **AI deployed without governance, methodology, and strategic discipline is.**

In the wrong hands, or in well-intentioned organizations without a system, it accelerates commoditization, erodes intellectual property, weakens brand trust, and collapses defensibility at unprecedented speed. What once required competitors years to copy, AI can now infer, approximate, and reproduce almost instantly.

While model builders have made extraordinary advances in capability, tooling, and data flywheels, the inner disciplines that historically protected enterprise value-quality, brand, strategic intent, and control are being dangerously marginalized.

That's the deeper strategic risk. The issue isn't simply that AI is powerful, or even that it's moving quickly. It's that the traditional disciplines that once slowed bad decisions, preserved soundness, and protected enterprise value are no longer sufficient when intelligence can grow at machine speed. Organizations now face a new requirement: they must translate hard-won strategic judgment into systems that can operate at the same speed as the technologies they're adopting.

This moment demands more than adoption. It demands **translation**. The 7i's methodology isn't being replaced by AI—it's being **ported into it.**

Each of the 7i's domains is being translated into a corresponding AI system encoded as decision logic, analytic frameworks, learning loops, and enforceable constraints. Together, these seven AI tools form the Moat Suite: a unified operating layer where the 7i's methodology lives on as executable intelligence rather than static guidance.

This isn't a cosmetic modernization of an existing framework. It's an architectural shift. A methodology that once guided people through interpretation, innovation, identify, investment, implementation, influence, and inspection is being reconstituted as a living system of decision logic, feedback loops, constraints, and institutional memory. The aim isn't to automate judgment away, but to preserve and extend it in a form that can be applied consistently, inspected rigorously, and improved continuously.

In this form, strategy becomes code. Brand becomes policy. Learning compounds advantage instead of leaking it.

This moment demands a **Systems** approach. This moment demands **AI moats**. Not models. Not features. That's why MoatWorks exists.

MoatWorks is the system-level answer to that requirement. It's designed not merely to add intelligence to the enterprise, but to organize intelligence so that it serves continuity, control, and compounding advantage. If AI is going to become an operating layer inside serious organizations, then it must be governed as seriously as finance, quality, brand, and risk. That's the threshold this guidebook is written to establish.

Governance Foundations

For an AI operating system to be credible inside large organizations, governance cannot be optional. It must be structural.

MoatWorks will incorporate several foundational governance mechanisms:

Decision Rights
Clear ownership over which decisions are automated, assisted, or human-approved.

Policy Enforcement
Identity, pricing, compliance, and strategic constraints translated into enforceable system rules.

Audit Trails

Persistent records of decisions, inputs, assumptions, and outcomes.

Model and Automation Monitoring

Detection of model drift, degraded decision quality, and unexpected behavior.

Escalation and Rollback Protocols

Mechanisms to pause, reverse, or redesign automated actions when thresholds are breached.

Governance is not an add-on to enterprise AI; it is part of what makes the system credible, controllable, and strategically durable. Combined with rigorous business strategy, quality disciplines, resilient architecture, and machine learning that strengthens with use, it helps create the conditions for data moats, improving offerings, economies of scale, network effects, higher switching costs, and stronger barriers to entry. In that form, AI becomes more than a toolset—it becomes a system for extending advantage while protecting the enterprise along the way.

Manufacturing Moats, Not Features

The Moat Factory, the company behind MoatWorks, exists for a specific purpose: to design, validate, and industrialize AI-powered businesses and platforms with durable competitive advantage. Its focus is not on tools, campaigns, or isolated use cases. It is on the manufacturing of moats: systems that improve with use, integrate more deeply into the real workings of an organization, and grow more difficult to replace as they accumulate learning, trust, and operational value. MoatWorks is the operating system created to make that possible.

Who This Publication Is For

First, let's be clear about who this guidebook is not for. It is not written for those seeking AI shortcuts, tool roundups, or tactical automation divorced from responsibility and long-term stewardship. AI can create activity almost instantly, but activity is not the same as advantage. This guidebook is written instead for organizations and leaders with the most to protect in an AI-accelerated world, especially those sitting on accumulated advantage such as intellectual property, brand trust, operational scale, market position, and institutional credibility built over decades. These assets remain powerful, but they also become more vulnerable when intelligence is deployed without structure, governance, or strategic discipline. AI can generate activity instantly.

This guidebook is about generating **advantage over time**.

Instead, this guidebook is written for organizations and leaders with the most to lose in an AI-accelerated world.

It's for those who sit on accumulated advantage: intellectual property, brand trust, operational scale, market position, and institutional credibility built over decades. These assets are powerful—but also increasingly vulnerable when intelligence is deployed without structure, governance, or strategic discipline.

Primary Audience

This work is intended for C-suite leaders, senior marketing and growth leaders, technology and enterprise architecture leaders, business and marketing analysts, and leaders within global systems integrators, consulting firms, technology services firms, and digital transformation organizations. It's intended for decision-makers and operators responsible for understanding where AI creates strategic leverage, how it becomes embedded into business systems, and how it can help a company become more adaptive, more defensible, and harder to displace over time.

Why This Audience Matters

Smaller organizations often adopt AI to gain leverage. Large organizations adopt AI to avoid erosion.

The paradox is that the organizations with the most data, brand equity, and operational scale are often the ones most exposed, because their systems were not designed for intelligence that learns, propagates, and compounds autonomously.

MoatWorks is designed to help these organizations **embed intelligence responsibly**, protect what matters, and turn AI from a force of dilution into a force of durable advantage.

Secondary Strategic Relevance

The ideas in this publication also have relevance for investors, software manufacturers, OEM and white-label partners, and potential acquirers evaluating companies that are building durable AI-enabled business systems. In that context, "increased switching costs" and "harder to displace over time" refers to strategic durability: deeper workflow integration, stronger learning loops, greater organizational dependence, and increased long-term enterprise value.

The Operating System Layer Most Organizations Lack

Most enterprise systems optimize functions: sales, marketing, finance, operations, etc. Few coordinate *decisions* across functions.

MoatWorks will sit above existing enterprise platforms, acting as a strategic coordination, intelligence, and inspection layer. It will unify seven persistent intelligent domains, each responsible for a distinct class of decision, learning loop, and system integration.

These domains are not phases. They're **continuous, circular, and collaborative processes**. Together, they form a closed-loop moat engine.

Why This Publication Comes First

Before an operating system can be trusted, its logic must be understood.

The chapters that follow introduce the worldview behind MoatWorks: how advantage is designed, how learning compounds, and why system-level orchestration — not isolated AI tools — is the true source of defensibility in the next era of enterprise.

3 | AI Domain—INTERPRET

Designing Shared Reality

See the system as intended, then as lived — so the right intelligence compounds.

Organizations don't fail because they lack data. They fail because they misread what the data means, overreact to the loudest signals, or move too quickly from observation to action without enough disciplined interpretation. In practice, this creates a familiar pattern: teams confuse activity with insight, strategy gets built on partial readings of the environment, and decisions are made before the enterprise has formed a coherent point of view. The first requirement of any serious operating system, then, isn't speed alone—it's interpretive clarity.

Why Interpretation Comes First

In an AI-saturated environment, speed is no longer a differentiator. Everyone can generate plans, content, forecasts, and analysis on demand. What differentiates organizations now is whether their actions *accumulate*.

Most don't.

They move quickly, but incoherently. Each initiative begins as if the last one never happened. Data is gathered, insights are generated, decisions are made—and then forgotten. When conditions change, the cycle restarts from zero.

This isn't a tooling problem. It's an **interpretation problem**.

INTERPRET is the domain responsible for establishing a shared reality inside the organization. It's where fragmented signals are converted into a common strategic baseline that persists over time. Without this function, AI amplifies noise. With it, learning compounds.

INTERPRET as a System Function (Not a Phase)

INTERPRET isn't a kickoff exercise or an annual diagnostic. It is a persistent system capability.

Its purpose is to continuously answer four questions: what is actually happening, what matters most now, which constraints are real versus assumed, and what must be decided next.

In MoatWorks, INTERPRET operates as the primary intake valve for proprietary context. It normalizes intelligence from across the enterprise—data, research, experience, and outcomes—into a coherent point of view that other domains can build upon.

What INTERPRET Produces

The output of INTERPRET is not a report. It is a real-time Strategic Point of View, fueled by AI business intelligence data feeders.

That point of view is concise enough to be shared across the organization. It is evidence-backed rather than aspirational, explicit about uncertainty, and clear about what will be done next.

It becomes the reference state for downstream decisions and is continuously refreshed as new outcomes are observed.

4 | AI Domain—INNOVATE

Designing Strategic Options Under Constraint

Innovation isn't idea generation. It's disciplined choice under real-world constraints.

Most organizations don't struggle because they have too few ideas. They struggle because ideas arrive disconnected from real constraints, strategic intent, and practical roads to value creation. Innovation then becomes either random brainstorming or expensive experimentation with no durable effect on the enterprise.

Over time, this creates fatigue, skepticism, and a widening gap between what sounds promising and what can actually strengthen advantage. It's why innovation has to be treated as a disciplined strategic function. Not the generation of novelty for its own sake, but the structured expansion of meaningful options the organization can evaluate, shape, and turn into defensible progress.

Why Innovation Must Be Engineered, Not Romanticized

Most organizations don't suffer from a lack of ideas. They suffer from an excess of unfiltered possibility. Backlogs accumulate faster than judgment can be applied.

AI amplifies this failure mode. When ideas are cheap to generate, discernment becomes the scarce capability.

INNOVATE exists to restore discipline.

INNOVATE as a Domain in the Operating System

Within MoatWorks, INNOVATE is a **planning and option-design domain** that sits directly downstream of INTERPRET.

Its role is to convert shared reality—market structure, capability truth, constraints, and intelligence, into a small number of strategically viable paths forward. These paths are not commitments. They're **designed options**.

What INNOVATE Produces

The output of INNOVATE is a rationalized portfolio of roadmaps and exploited gap-opportunity options, each shaped not simply by possibility, but by strategic discipline. Every option is defined by its intended scope, the capabilities and dependencies required to pursue it, the learning it is expected to produce, and the measurable signals that can validate whether it is working. Each is also examined for downside exposure, reversibility, and the conditions that would justify escalation or abandonment. INNOVATE sets the stage. What follows determines whether advantage becomes legible.

5 | AI Domain—IDENTIFY

Strategic Branding as a Compounding Strategic Asset

IDENTIFY is the long-term architecture of value, trust, and leadership.

Organizations don't lose relevance all at once. They lose it gradually, as clarity about who they are and what they uniquely mean begins to erode under the pressure of growth, imitation, and constant market noise. Messaging starts to drift, differentiation softens, internal decisions lose a common anchor, and the enterprise becomes easier to compare, substitute, or misunderstand. That's why IDENTIFY can't be treated as a surface-level branding exercise. It has to function as a strategic discipline that protects consistency, sharpens distinction, and ensures that as the organization evolves, it doesn't become less itself in the process.

Why IDENTIFY Determines Long-Term Outcomes

IDENTIFY is the most underestimated domain in the system precisely because its returns compound quietly over time. When done correctly and nurtured consistently, it increases pricing power, accelerates adoption, improves resilience during disruption, and materially enhances enterprise and resale value.

This is how organizations move *up and to the right*: improving capabilities while simultaneously increasing scale, authority, and category leadership.

Identity Is More Than Packaging

Visual identity and branding matter, but it is not the essence of IDENTIFY. IDENTIFY is the disciplined, consistent articulation of what an organization stands for, what it refuses to become, the problems it chooses to solve, the trade-offs it is willing to defend, and the experience customers can count on. It is less about surface expression and more about strategic clarity made durable and repeatable.

In that sense, this domain serves as the blueprint of the organization's core. As conditions change, IDENTIFY remains the reference point against which strategy is tested again and again, helping ensure that adaptation does not come at the cost of coherence.

Brand Architecture, Voice, and Naming Discipline

Two practical IDENTIFY disciplines matter more than

most organizations admit:

> **Taxonomy and architecture:** how offerings, capabilities, and benefits are named and organized into an understandable system. This is how distinct value becomes legible at scale.

> **Voice and tone:** the consistent expression of intent across channels, sales motions, product experiences, and executive communication.

Identity must also be **exportable**—understandable across regions, cultures, and stakeholder contexts. If it requires explanation to function, it will fail under speed.

Experience-Led

IDENTIFY becomes real through experience. Exposure isn't experience.

Experience is the repeated alignment between promise and delivery. When that alignment is sustained, it produces trust—and trust is required to build and enrich moats.

The Storyteller Function

The Storyteller function is accountable for consistency, not cosmetics. Its role is to capture and express the organization's innermost value in a way that remains true as the business grows. It translates strategy into meaning customers can understand, ensures that what is promised aligns with what people actually experience, and protects the integrity of the narrative from drifting into exaggeration or confusion.

At its best, this function helps the organization say the

same essential truth across every touchpoint without becoming repetitive or superficial. As the company scales, the Storyteller preserves coherence, making sure the story remains credible, recognizable, and rooted in lived reality rather than surface polish.

Organizational Culture as the Internal Mirror

Identity must be mirrored internally to be credible externally. Culture isn't perks; it's the behavior the organization rewards and tolerates. When identity and culture diverge, influence becomes persuasion without trust.

Why IDENTIFY Comes Before INVEST

Investment without identity produces dilution.

Only when an organization is clear about who it is, and who it intends to become, can it invest with conviction rather than caution.

6 | AI Domain—INVEST

Turning Value into Market-Shaping Commitment

INVEST isn't pricing mechanics. It's conviction, signaling, and customer buy-in.

Most organizations don't fail because they never invest. They fail because they invest without enough clarity about where advantage is actually forming, what should be reinforced, and which opportunities only appear attractive because they're urgent, fashionable, or politically easy to approve. Resources get spread across too many initiatives, strong points of view get replaced by compromise, and capital moves faster than strategic understanding. That's why investment can't be treated as budgeting alone. It has to function as a disciplined allocation of attention, capital, and commitment toward the choices most likely to strengthen the system, deepen differentiation, and produce compounding returns over time.

In this domain, economics, market reality, and strategic intent converge.

It's where economies of scale, demand versus supply, and what a market will bear meet a continuously learning system that reasons forward—creating value beyond competitors and beyond price.

Markets signal willingness to pay, elasticity, and competitive pressure. They don't define leadership.

Organizations that price only to what the market will bear eventually converge toward sameness.

INVEST exists to break that gravity.

Within MoatWorks, INVEST is a living domain that continuously reads market signals, cost structures, demand patterns, and customer outcomes and then resolves how to create value above the rest.

When done correctly, INVEST reshapes the customer's own economics. It enables customers to change their jobs to be done—their workflows, priorities, and outcomes—in ways that materially improve their business or lives.

At that point, customers are no longer merely buying. They're investing.

This is where pricing transforms into commitment, loyalty replaces comparison, and value creation becomes self-reinforcing.

INVEST isn't about extracting more from the market. It's about creating so much differentiated value that customers willingly invest in you as a supplier, partner, and platform.

Why Markets Rarely Lead

Markets don't reliably articulate what they'll value next. Category leaders shape demand by teaching customers what to value.

Investment decisions determine whether an organization participates in a category or leads it.

Customers as Investors

The objective isn't to price at what the market can accommodate; it's to price and allocate in ways that cause customers to feel they're **investing in you**, because the value you provide is meaningfully better, more reliable, and more consequential than alternatives.

This dynamic occurs when your value changes customer behavior and reshapes their "jobs to be done." When you alter the customer's day, workflow, or outcomes, price becomes secondary and commitment becomes natural.

Beyond Legacy Pricing Frames

INVEST extends well beyond the outdated idea that pricing is just one lever. It includes pricing strategy and margin architecture, but also the broader economic structure of the business: reducing total cost of ownership, allocating resources in the right sequence, protecting focus by weighing opportunity cost, and sending clear strategic signals to the market.

In that sense, INVEST is about shaping how value is captured, defended, and communicated. It ensures that financial decisions are not made in isolation, but as part of a coherent leadership agenda that strengthens margins, sharpens priorities, and reinforces the organization's position over time.

TCO, ROI, and Total Return on Impact

Return on investment (ROI) matters, but it often focuses too much on quick results and high volume.

Thinking in terms of Total Cost of Ownership (TCO) offers a longer horizon. It positions your offering as a better system for the customer, not a cheaper transaction.

A practical extension of this thinking is total return on impact: the downstream value your offering creates beyond the immediate ROI calculation. When you understand the second and third order outcomes you enable for customers, you are in a stronger position to justify premium pricing with integrity, because the value being delivered is broader and more enduring than the first transaction alone might suggest.

That same understanding also sharpens strategic judgment. It helps you prioritize the capabilities most likely to unlock future value and gives you a clearer basis for expanding into new segments without losing coherence. Rather than chasing adjacent opportunities randomly, you grow from a deeper grasp of the full impact your offering creates.

The Catalyst Function

The Catalyst function ensures that investment decisions are deliberate rather than habitual, concentrated rather than diluted, and aligned with long-term leadership goals. Its purpose is to bring discipline to capital allocation, so resources are not scattered across familiar patterns or politically convenient choices, but directed toward the few priorities most capable of creating lasting advantage.

In doing so, Catalyst protects the organization from two common failures: underpricing real value and overfunding mediocrity. It helps leaders invest with clarity, defend focus, and resist the tendency to spread resources too thinly across efforts that do not meaningfully strengthen the business.

7 | AI Domain—IMPLEMENT

Embedding Strategy into Operational Reality

Strategy becomes real when it's embedded into systems, people, and workflows.

Most organizations don't break down at the level of resolution. They break down in the handoff between decision and execution, where strategy meets process, ownership, constraints, and everyday reality. What looked logical at the planning stage can quickly fragment once teams interpret priorities differently, workflows fail to align, or execution proceeds without enough connection to the original strategic logic.

That's why implementation can't be treated as rollout alone. It has to function as the disciplined embedment of strategy into real operations so that what the organization intends to do is actually carried through in a form that's consistent, accountable, and sustainable.

Why IMPLEMENT Is Where Moats Are Actually Built

Most strategies fail not because they're poorly conceived, but because they're poorly installed.

IMPLEMENT is the domain responsible for turning intent into operational gravity, making the chosen strategy the organization's default behavior of the organization rather than an aspiration.

This is where switching costs are deliberately created and governed—balancing strategic, sustained value against the need for ongoing adaptability.

Working Backward from the Customer Experience

Implementation begins by working backward from the experience you want customers to have. Starting with the customer experience as the anchor, the organization then designs the operational system required to deliver that experience consistently and reliably. This means choosing channels and routes to market—direct, partner, or hybrid—based not on convenience alone, but on which model best preserves the intended experience.

From there, implementation extends into the supporting structure that makes the promise real: supply chain and fulfillment systems that protect reliability, CRM and customer intelligence systems that sustain relationships, and service models that govern enablement, onboarding, support, and retention. In other words, implementation is where desired experience is translated into repeatable operational design.

Human Capital as Infrastructure

People are not an afterthought in IMPLEMENT; they are part of the infrastructure itself. Successful implementation depends on clear role definition and accountability, training and enablement that are aligned with strategy, incentives that reinforce the behaviors the organization actually wants, and a realistic capacity model for delivering at scale. Without those elements, even a sound strategy can break down in execution.

In other words, implementation is not complete when systems and processes are designed. It is only complete when the people responsible for carrying them out are equipped, aligned, and structured to perform consistently as the organization grows.

The Enabler Function

The Enabler function is responsible for operational coherence. It ensures that the right platforms are selected and integrated, that systems communicate in ways that reinforce rather than undermine one another, and that processes remain aligned with strategic intent. Its role is not simply to install tools, but to create an environment in which the organization can function as a coordinated whole.

When this function is working well, friction is reduced for both customers and employees. Interactions become smoother, handoffs become clearer, and the operating model begins to support the strategy instead of obstructing it. In that sense, the Enabler helps turn complexity into usable structure.

Why IMPLEMENT Precedes INFLUENCE

Influence without implementation creates promises the organization can't keep.

IMPLEMENT ensures that when the organization goes to market, it can deliver—consistently, reliably, and at scale.

8 | AI Domain—INFLUENCE

Turning Value into Adoption, Belief, and Demand

INFLUENCE is where value meets the market and where many organizations mistakenly think marketing begins and ends.

Most organizations don't struggle because they have nothing to say. They struggle because even strong ideas fail to travel with enough clarity, credibility, and force to shape decisions beyond the team that produced them. Messages get diluted, stakeholders interpret the same strategy differently, and important initiatives lose momentum because alignment was assumed rather than built. That's why influence can't be treated as communication alone. It has to function as a strategic discipline that translates intent into shared conviction, earns trust across stakeholders, and gives the organization the ability to move important decisions forward with coherence rather than confusion.

Influence Is Not the Whole System

INFLUENCE is often viewed as synonymous with marketing. That framing is incomplete.

INFLUENCE isn't the source of value. It's the amplifier of value that already exists. When influence is relied on to compensate for weak interpretation, unclear identity, poor investment choices, or broken implementation, it inevitably overpromises and underdelivers.

What INFLUENCE Does

INFLUENCE is the domain responsible for shaping behavior, adoption, and belief. It is persuasion and inspiration tied to reality: igniting interest, inciting action, and promoting value through credible calls to action. In practical terms, it builds top-of-funnel opportunity and demand flow by increasing awareness and consideration, establishing trust, nurturing marketing qualified leads (MQLs), and converting them into sales qualified leads (SQLs) and revenue motion.

But MQLs and SQLs are indicators, not the purpose. The real purpose of INFLUENCE is belief formation that converts. Its job is to create understanding and confidence strong enough to move people from attention to action, and from action to enduring commercial value.

Channels as Trust Infrastructure

Channels are not merely distribution mechanisms; they are trust infrastructure. Every channel either strengthens credibility or weakens it. For that reason, INFLUENCE is responsible for ensuring that channel choice reflects actual customer behavior and context, that messaging remains consistent across touchpoints, and that sales enablement stays anchored in strategic truth rather than improvised claims.

When those elements are aligned, the organization does more than distribute messages efficiently. It builds confidence in a way that feels coherent and credible, so each interaction reinforces belief instead of creating doubt.

AI's Role in INFLUENCE

AI strengthens influence when it is used responsibly to personalize messaging at scale, optimize timing and sequencing, and detect meaningful engagement patterns. Used well, it can make communication more relevant, timelier, and more responsive without losing strategic discipline.

But influence without ethics degrades trust. AI should support judgment, not replace it. The moment automation begins to override discernment, persuasion becomes manipulation and credibility begins to erode.

9 | AI Domain—INSPECT

Benefit Realization and Continuous Advantage

INSPECT is where strategy proves itself—or quietly fails. It represents the Optimization and renewal phase of digital transformation, the point where strategy is tested against reality and either compounds or erodes.

Most organizations don't lose advantage in one dramatic moment. They lose it gradually, as performance drifts, assumptions go untested, benefits go unmeasured, and early gains are mistaken for lasting progress. What was once a strong initiative can slowly weaken if no disciplined mechanism exists to review outcomes, detect degradation, and decide where renewal is needed next. That's why inspection can't be treated as an after-the-fact audit alone. It must function as a strategic discipline that measures realized value, surfaces drift before it becomes decline and turns execution back into learning so the organization can sustain advantage rather than merely declare it.

Benefit Realization, Not Reporting

Most organizations measure performance. Very few learn from it.

INSPECT is the domain responsible for benefit realization—ensuring that effort, spend, and attention translate into measurable outcomes, and that those outcomes feed forward into better decisions.

This discipline aligns with formal Benefits Realization Management (BRM): value must be defined in advance, measured after deployment, reconciled against original intent, and translated into financial and strategic impact. If value can't be demonstrated against the original investment thesis, the system must adjust.

Dashboards are not the output. Decisions are.

What INSPECT Measures

KPIs are necessary, but they are not enough. INSPECT is the domain that evaluates outcomes against original intent, asking not only what happened, but whether what happened actually strengthened the position the organization was trying to build. That evaluation includes the obvious commercial and operating measures such as revenue and margin impact, acquisition efficiency, funnel health, advertising ROI, demand quality, retention, expansion, lifetime value, brand lift, mindshare, trust durability, and overall operational efficiency and scalability.

But INSPECT goes further than performance reporting. It distinguishes between visible progress and meaningful progress. A result can look positive in the short term and still weaken long-term advantage if it degrades trust, narrows margins, creates fragility, or pulls the organization away from its strategic intent. For that reason, INSPECT is not simply a dashboard function. It is a discipline of interpretation, testing whether outcomes are truly compounding or only temporarily flattering.

In AI-enabled systems, INSPECT also has to monitor the integrity of decisions and models embedded in operations. That includes watching for model drift, data distribution shifts, declining prediction accuracy, degrading confidence, rising automation failure rates, and the gradual deterioration of decision quality over time. These systems are not static assets. They are statistical engines operating inside real business conditions, and those conditions change continuously.

Without ongoing monitoring, AI systems do not usually fail loudly at first; they decay quietly. Performance can erode in ways that are subtle enough to escape immediate notice but serious enough to distort decisions, weaken execution, and create false confidence. That is why INSPECT must evaluate not only business outcomes, but also the health of the intelligence systems influencing them.

Ultimately, a short-term win that weakens long-term position does not pass the INSPECT test. The purpose of this domain is to ensure that what appears to be working is actually strengthening the organization in a durable way.

Continuous Performance Improvement

INSPECT institutionalizes improvement by turning

evaluation into a repeatable discipline. Its role is to help the organization detect drift as early as possible, determine which levers are actually moving outcomes, retire what is no longer working, and double down where advantage is beginning to compound. In that sense, INSPECT is not just about reviewing results. It is about creating a structured way for the business to learn, refine, and strengthen itself over time.

Each inspection cycle should end with a small number of specific improvements that will be implemented next. That practical step is essential. Inspection without action is theater, because observation alone does not create progress. The value of INSPECT lies in its ability to convert insight into disciplined change.

Reinvestment and Strategic Refresh

Inspection is incomplete unless it informs reinvestment. Each cycle should explicitly determine whether the organization is capturing the value it expected, what is breaking, drifting, or degrading, and where capital, attention, or capability should be reallocated. Without that discipline, inspection becomes passive observation rather than strategic control.

INSPECT exists to feed the INVEST and INNOVATE phases. It helps determine whether the right move is to double down, recalibrate, retire, or redesign. Even successful systems can stagnate when reinvestment is absent or misdirected, so the real purpose of inspection is not just to measure performance, but to direct what happens next.

AI's Role in INSPECT

AI strengthens INSPECT by making monitoring more continuous, anomaly detection more sensitive, and insight generation faster and more scalable. It can surface trend shifts earlier, highlight weak signals that human teams might miss, and shorten the feedback loop between action and consequence. Used properly, it increases visibility and helps organizations respond with greater speed and precision.

But AI does not decide what matters. That remains a leadership judgment. Its value lies in accelerating awareness, not replacing interpretation. INSPECT still depends on humans to determine which signals deserve attention, which changes are meaningful, and what action should follow.

Closing the Loop

INSPECT feeds directly back into INTERPRET, closing the loop between results and understanding. Each cycle deepens shared reality across the organization, sharpens innovation, clarifies identity, improves investment discipline, tightens implementation, and strengthens influence. What is learned does not remain isolated in reporting; it becomes input for better judgment across the entire system.

The goal is not perfection. The goal is compounding progress. Over time, that accumulation of better decisions, clearer signals, and more disciplined adjustment is what turns transformation from a one-time program into a self-renewing system. That is the difference between motion and advantage.

10 | Conclusion:

Before the Code, the System

AI isn't the first technology to promise transformation, and it won't be the last. What makes this moment different isn't the power of the tools, but the speed at which ungoverned intelligence can erode value, trust, and differentiation.

History has already shown us what works: disciplined systems, continuous learning, quality embedded into operations, and brands built on consistency rather than spectacle.

MoatWorks intends to carry those lessons forward at AI speed.

This guidebook was written before the code for a reason. Systems must be understood before they're automated. Advantage must be designed before it's scaled. Moats must be built intentionally, not discovered accidentally.

The chapters you have just read describe a closed-loop operating system for growth, innovation, and trust — one that learns, adapts, and compounds rather than resets.

The future will reward those who embed intelligence responsibly, protect what matters, and invest in systems that endure.

That's ultimately the wager behind this primer. Not that every organization will build the same system, or move at the same pace, or express advantage in the same way. But that the next era will belong to those who treat intelligence not as a shortcut, but as an operating responsibility.

The winners won't be the ones who generate the most activity. They'll be the ones who stay consistent under pressure, convert learning into the enterprise's collective know-how, and build structures capable of compounding judgment rather than merely accelerating output.

Because that's what a moat becomes in an AI-saturated world: not a static asset, but a living system of interpretation, identity, innovation, investment, implementation, influence, and inspection held together by governance, continuity, and design. If this guidebook has done its job, it has made that system visible before it becomes executable.

The code comes next.

About the Author

John Michael Kostak is Founder & CEO of US Digital Works and The Moat Factory. A marketing and growth strategist with more than 30+ years of experience, he has worked across Silicon Valley, Boston, and Washington, D.C., helping organizations build, modernize, and sustain powerful brands and digital footprints.

Over the course of his career, John has operated at the intersection of business strategy, marketing, innovation, and transformation—guiding companies through periods of growth, reinvention, and increasing technological complexity. He's the creator of the trademarked 7i's Marketing System, a strategic framework designed to help leaders interpret change, identify opportunity, and build durable advantage in fast-moving markets.

In Before the Code, John brings together decades of experience in strategy, branding, and operating discipline to argue that lasting advantage in the AI era will not come from tools alone, but from the systems that govern how intelligence is applied, trusted, and improved over time.

Proceeds from the sale of this book will benefit
Jacob's Ladder at Brookside Farm

www.jacobsladderbrookside.com

www.ingramcontent.com/pod-product-compliance
Lightning Source LLC
Chambersburg PA
CBHW061132160726
48006CB00036B/1782